THIS BOOK BELONG'S TO

Phone Number

Address

If you find this book anywhere, please return it to the address above

Things you should know about domestic animals

Top 5

Various information for children as well as pet lovers

Pets are animals that humans can keep for mutual enjoyment between them and other ends, so the relationship between them represents a symbiotic relationship, raising pets is present from prehistoric times to the present time, and it is among the most famous animals that are bred Horses, cats and dogs.

dogs were the first animals that were bred, while horses are believed to have been domesticated in the ancient stone age or in the modern stone age, while cats were domesticated as a pet in the era of the modern kingdom in Egypt, and are now the most popular among pets

Dogs

Dogs are loyal animals to their owner, they work to protect and accompany him , provide many services to him, and in turn, the person must be loyal to his dog and take care of him and his health well, morever pictures of caring for dogs to take care of their food and drink; Contrary to what is believed, dogs cannot eat all kinds of food that a person eats. Its digestive system is different from the digestive system of a person, as there are some types of food that he cannot digest, and some of them are toxic to him.

You can Feed domestic dogs boiled eggs, as well as a small amount of fruits, such as slices of apples, paying attention not to include any seeds because they may be toxic to the dog. Pistachios and unsalted peanut butter are considered two types of food that are useful for dogs, as they contain a high percentage of protein and nutrients important to his health such as fat, however they should be given to him only in small quantities, Yogurt and cheese are good foods for dogs because they contain calcium, protein and good nutrients.

Dogs use body language to communicate with each other, and this language includes certain expressions of the face and movement of the tail specifically lifting it, in addition to individual ears when standing, for example when the dog feels fear, the parking of his body hair is an indication of his fear or even his discomfort, and when he is aggressive it shows his teeth He relaxes his ears and straightens his tail.

Feed the puppies

⭐ **Apply the veterinarian's instructions, or the instructions written in ready-to-eat food packages, and do not over-feed puppies so that they do not gain excess weight.**

⭐ **Introducing new food to the pups gradually, by mixing the new food with the old food for two weeks, then gradually increasing its amount; Until the puppy gets used to it and does not get any complications.**

Arrange the timing of eating, provided that the small puppies are fed three times a day, the older puppy twice, and only provide one meal for adult dogs.

Cats

Cats are mammals, which are small animals, and pets that are raised for fun and for catching rodents, and there are about 60 different types of cats that are recognized, and cats have a flexible body and fast reactions and claws that can kill their prey, They also have sharp teeth and a good sense of smell and have the ability to see at night.

cats are social animals that communicate by making sounds or by using their own body language, and have an average length of about 46 cm from head to body and height from 23 cm to 25 cm Domestic cats typically weigh 4 to 5 kg, and males are usually larger than female.

Did you know

- Most cats prefer to use the left paw.
- Cats greet each other by touching their noses.
- Cats sleep for 12 or 13 hours a day.
- Chocolate is fatal to cats because it contains theobromine.

- Cats can form about 100 different types of sounds.
- Cats cannot taste sweet.
- Cat brains are 90% similar to human brains.
- Cats can move their ears up to 180 degrees

- Cats have nearly 30 sharp teeth in their mouths.

- Cat eyes have a reflective layer, which amplifies the light, thus seeing the object better, and is 6 times clearer when the light is down.

- Cats share dogs with the third eyelid, which is the membrane in the inner corner of the eye, and is an additional protective device for the eye.

- The cat's ear contains about 32 muscles, while the human ear contains only 12 muscles, and thus the cat's ear muscles help it to locate the prey. The cat has a prickly tongue.

- Cats cannot focus, seeing things that are 30 centimeters or more closer to them; This is because she has big eyes.

- Cats do not prefer milk, nor any dairy product.

- Cats kept at home live longer than those on the street.

Rabbits

Rabbits are very intelligent, inquisitive animals and come in a variety of breeds, shapes and sizes. Each rabbit has its own unique personality, and it typically lives for between 7 and 12 years.

the rabbit can be shy, lazy, stubborn, or even fierce, and the lack of awareness of most people of this matter is considered to be the reason for getting rid of some rabbits when they reach them, as their strong and indépendant personality is formed.

Rabbits can be raised within the home as farm animals, as it is considered relatively easy and has multiple benefits; Individuals can raise these animals at home without causing inconvenience to their neighbors, as rabbits are characterized by being odorless and calm, and they are easy to guide and dirty animals, in addition to that their droppings are a useful fertilizer for the garden of the house.

Some of the health symptoms that may appear on the rabbit are spots that spread inside the ears, diarrhea or secretions from the nose or eye, and the health condition must also be monitored For rabbit teeth, dental problems are common among rabbits, and although rabbits do not need many vaccines, there are some important vaccines to protect them from deadly diseases such as Viral Haemorrhagic Disease, which is known as VHD.

You should consult your veterinarian to learn about rabbit vaccines and the number of vaccinations, and you should pay attention to its temperature. The average temperature of rabbits is between 38.5 and 40 degrees Celsius, and the rate of her heartbeat if she is not exposed to stress ranges between 180 to 250 beats in One minute.

Knowing the correct way to feed rabbits is very important, as diseases caused by malnutrition are the most prevalent among rabbits, so care must be taken to develop a healthy diet for them as any blockage in their digestive system can cause major health risks. The rabbit should not eat food for 12 to 24 hours, so it should be brought to the attention of the specialist veterinarian immediately, although rabbits are distinguished as herbivores, that is, they eat plants, but this does not prevent them from eating some other foods such as roots, worms, snails and tree bark, and it is worth noting That rabbits use the sense of smell to identify food and its location, due to the rabbit's inability to see what is directly in front of it

Young rabbits do not need nutrition during the first twenty days of their lives, they depend entirely on breast milk for that period, and after more than two weeks of age, young children start to leave their place to start gradually eating herbs along with the mother's milk, which is less dependent Gradually until they are completely weaned and begin to rely on green fodder, vegetables and other nutritious foods

Hamster

The hamster is considered a rodent that is characterized by its short, full legs, its short tail, and its small ears. The size of the hamster varies from one type to the other, as its length varies according to its type from approximately 5 - 34 cm. As for the color of the fur of hamsters, it varies from one type to another; There are hamsters with black, white, gray, brown, yellow, or red fur. There are also species of multicolored fur.

TIPS

❑Feeding hamsters daily; It is one of the animals that loves to eat and preserves food at the same time, a person may find a hidden amount of food under the wood shavings, and in the hamster's mouth.

❑Always provide water in the cage; The hamster does not drink a large amount of water, but does drink as soon as he feels thirsty.

❑Buy hamster food at pet stores.

❑Distribute the food on the cage floor and hide it in the corners and games in it.

❑Avoid giving him human food, as it may affect him and cause him some health problems.

❑Putting food away from the place designated for urination and defecation.

❑Providing small amounts of food to the hamster each time, to be able to monitor whether it is sensitive to a specific type of food.

❑Dispose of the extra food after the hamster has finished eating, so that he does not collect it under the sleeping area.

❑Wash the fruits and vegetables thoroughly before serving them to the hamster, and remove the seeds from the fruit.

❑Take the vegetables and fruits out of the refrigerator well in advance so that their temperature is close to the room temperature when served to the hamster.

❑Ensure that ready-made foods for hamsters constitute half of the daily food ration for hamsters, provided that a good quality is selected that contains all the nutrients and vitamins that he needs, And Turkeys to supply adequate protein.

❑Serve some biscuits or slices of bread, dog food or parrot as a hamster snack, and make sure to cut them into small pieces beforehand.

Food prohibited to be served to hamsters

There are some types of foods that are prohibited from serving hamsters because they are difficult to digest and may lead to intestinal disorders. Including: avocado, orange, lemon, garlic, onions, parsley, celery, thyme oregano, basil, radish, uncooked beans, chocolate, and sugar. It is also prohibited to provide food prepared for humans for hamsters because it contains a high percentage of fat and salt, and some can be served Types of foods such as grapes, carrots, and beets once or twice a week, but in small quantities.

Parrots

The diversity of birds in their beautiful shapes, the most famous of which is the parrot, which is one of the spoiled birds that a person loves and reared by humans, as it is distinguished by its yellow, red, blue, and green colors, and its large head and claws that help it hang on the trees of forests, and its ability to imitate sounds

What distinguishes him most is that he is a faithful bird, that is, he does not marry a male over his female, and socially familiar and befriends those who raise him, and to raise a budgie in homes like any bird, there must be conditions and care for his breeding to succeed in the home, and you must know the type of budgie that the person acquires in order to follow the correct method of breeding.

When buying a parrot and bringing it home the first thing that the bird feels is fear of the new environment as well as from the people around him, and to break this fear of the bird must accustom him to the people of the house and stop his voice that indicates his fear, and it is preferable to place his cage in the center of the house and not to gather around and disturb him with loud sounds After a while,

 he will get to know the people of the house and feel reassured, and during this period the food is served continuously so that he is ready to eat and prefers to serve the peanuts to avoid continuous hunger.

A parrot loves companionship in the cage just like any other living creature. When owning a parrot , the male and female must be available in the cage itself.

Attention must be given to providing clean food for this bird, as he loves to eat grains, vegetables and fruits, and drinking water should not be neglected and it is advisable to change it continuously to keep it clean.

The parrot are medium-sized birds, and for this the cage must be large in order to move freely and place a wooden beam to stand and sit on it, and keep it clean constantly.

do not put him under the spray with a strong current but under Normal water, and upon drying it dries alone, that is, do not use the towel, and not to put it in the sun until it dries, and therefore it is advised to keep it away from direct air currents and heat of the conditioner so that it does not become infected and diseases, and during that the cage is cleaned well until the budgie feels comfortable

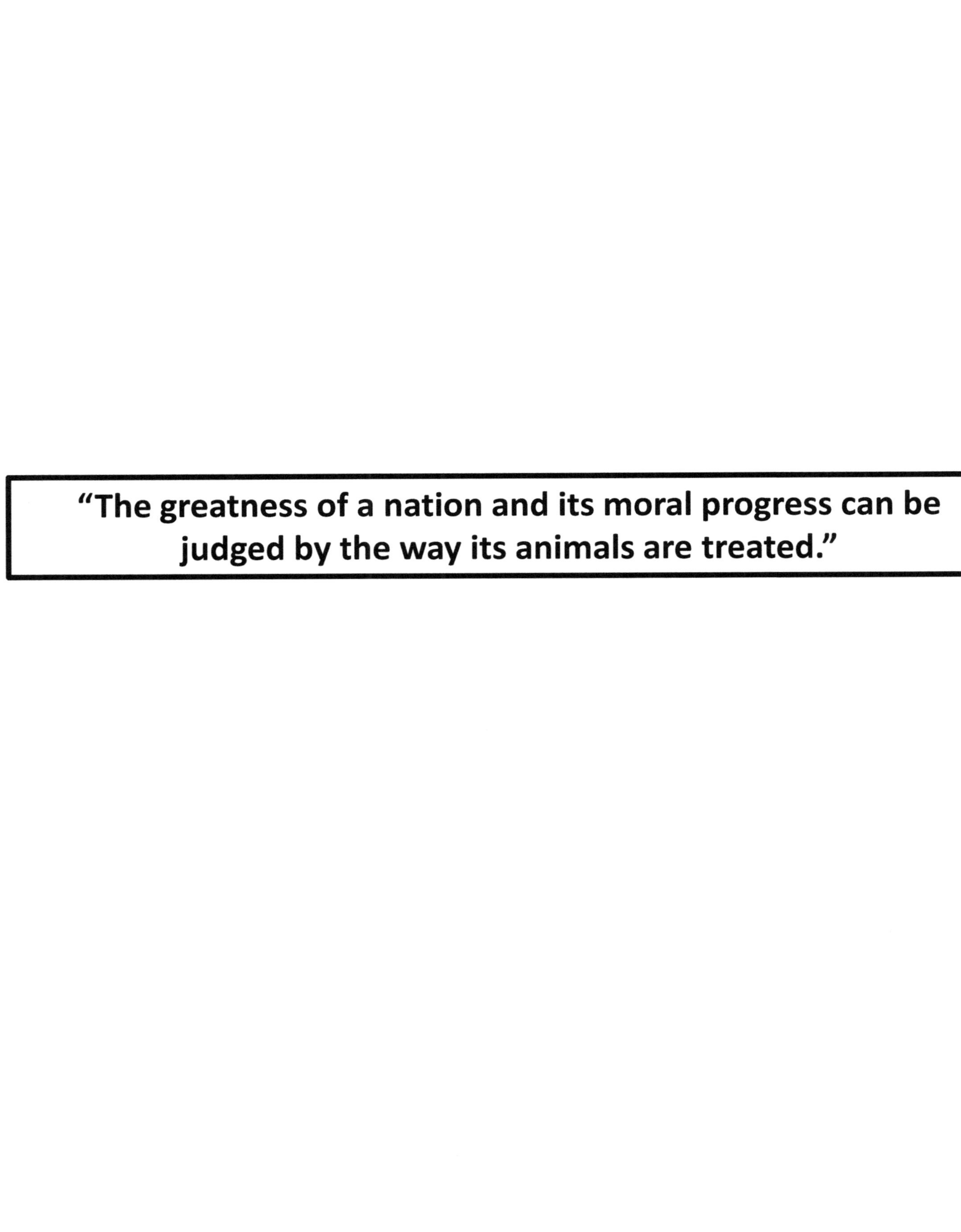

"The greatness of a nation and its moral progress can be judged by the way its animals are treated."